T🐾P 50
KINGS & QUEENS

T☻P 50 KINGS & QUEENS

TERRY DEARY

Illustrated by
MARTIN BROWN

◢ SCHOLASTIC

Scholastic Children's Books,
Euston House, 24 Eversholt Street,
London NW1 1DB, UK

A division of Scholastic Ltd
London ~ New York ~ Toronto ~ Sydney ~ Auckland
Mexico City ~ New Delhi ~ Hong Kong

First published in the UK by Scholastic Ltd, 2015
This edition published 2017

Text © Terry Deary, 2015
Illustration © Martin Brown, 2015
Colour by Rob Davis

ISBN 978 1407 17942 1

Printed and bound by Toppan Leefung Printing Limited

2 4 6 8 10 9 7 5 3 1

www.scholastic.co.uk

CONTENTS

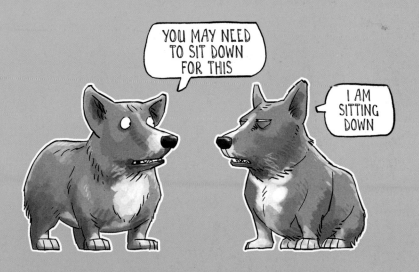

INTRODUCTION

Britain has been ruled by some weird people. You could look at the throne in any age and see some of the cruellest kings and quaintest queens in the history of the world.

There was the queen who chopped off the hands of writers who wrote rude things about her. **Cruel.**

THERE GOES PICKING MY NOSE

There was the king who had you hanged for playing the bagpipes. **Batty.**
There were kings who had their enemies beheaded. **Ruthless.**
And quite a few who had their friends or family executed. **Nasty.**
The tales of these terrible people are endless.

WHAT A BEASTLY BUNCH
WHAT A GRUESOME GANG
WHAT A PUTRID P—

CHOP!

OUCH

In 1066 William the Conqueror and his Normans bashed the Brits. There have been more than 40 miserable monarchs since then.

Here's a rotten rhyme to help you remember them all:

> Willie, Willie, Harry, Stee,
> Harry, Dick, John, Harry Three;
> One, two, three Neds, Richard Two
> Harrys Four, Five, Six ... then who?
> Edwards Four, Five, Dick the bad,
> Harrys twain VII VIII and Ned the Lad;
> Mary, Bessie, James the Vain,
> Charlie, Charlie, James again ...
> William and Mary, Anna Gloria,
> Four Georges I II III IV, William and Victoria;
> Edward Seven next, and then
> George the Fifth in 1910;
> Ned the Eighth soon abdicated
> Then George the Sixth was coronated;
> Now it's Liz, then we'll arrive ...
> At Charlie Three, then William Five.

The people of the islands had rulers before William the Conqueror arrived with his nasty Normans. Throw in a few of those and we have a nice round 50. The vile verses above tell you their names, but maybe some more potty poems will help you to remember the interesting bits about each one. The important bits, the funny bits and, of course, the horrible bits.

What we need is a *Horrible Histories* book of our 50 Kings and Queens. Amazing but true ... you are reading it right now!
Read on ...

BOUDICA
(died AD 61)

The Romans invaded Britain and took over the south – the bit we call England now. Some of the old Brit kings and queens fought to free themselves – queens like Boudica.

Famous for ...

... revolting! The Romans robbed Boudica's Iceni tribe and flogged her. So in AD 61 she gathered an army and fought back. Her tribe attacked the Roman camps and murdered all the men, women and children they found there.

FOUL FACTS

✹ Boudica was extra cruel to the Roman women. She pushed a pointed pole through many of them, then hoisted them up to die.

✹ The Romans met the Iceni in a battle, and the Iceni brought their families along to watch. The families watched from a line of wagons at the back. The Romans drove Boudica's fighters back to the wall of wagons. The trapped fighters and their families were slaughtered: 80,000 Iceni died but only 400 Romans.

✹ Boudica didn't want to be a Roman slave so she took poison and died. Some say her body lies under Platform 8 of King's Cross Station in London.

Potty poem

Red-haired, angry, wild and mean,
Bou-di-ca the warrior queen.
Slaughtered Romans in their beds,
Lost in battle. Poison. Dead.

10

BOUDICA

TOP 50

COEL HEN

(AD 350–420)

After the Romans had ruled England and Wales for 400 years, they left. A lot of British chiefs and their tribes took over the land they left behind. In the north, the top king was King Coel.

★ England was being invaded by pagans – they weren't Christians like King Coel and his family. Coel's son, Ceneu, led the fight against the invaders. He invited the Saxons (from Germany) to help. A b-i-g mistake. The Saxons liked England. They would be back ... not to fight for Coel Hen's family, but to attack them!

Famous for ...

... his age. 'Hen' meant 'Old', so he was 'Old' King Coel. The nursery rhyme, 'Old King Cole', might have been written about him.

FOUL FACTS

★ Some old books say Coel was the great grandfather of the famous King Arthur – the legendary king who ruled the Knights of the Round Table.

Potty poem

Old King Cole was a worried old soul
And a worried old soul was he.
He called for the Saxons to fight in his wars
And they laughed, 'This land's for me.'
Every Saxon had a fine axe, and a very fine Saxon sword;
Now there's none so scared as can compare
With King Cole and the Saxon hordes.

VORTIGERN

When the Romans left Britain and King Coel and his family ruled in the north, King Vortigern ruled in the south.

What's his **story?**

Vortigern tried to be too clever. He had enemies all around, but he thought he could get one enemy to fight his other enemy so they would both leave him alone.

The Irish were attacking Vortigern's lands in North Wales. He let warrior chief Cunedda and his Gododdin tribe settle in North Wales. Cunedda could fight off the Irish. It worked.

So who would help him fight off the Scots from the north? He invited the Saxon bullies Hengist and Horsa to help him fight them, and this is where things all went horribly wrong. A monk called Gildas told the story …

TO HOLD BACK THE PICT ENEMIES FROM SCOTLAND HE BROUGHT IN THOSE VILE, UNSPEAKABLE SAXONS, LED BY BROTHERS HENGIST AND HORSA. THESE SAXONS ARE HATED BY GOD AND HUMANS ALIKE. NOTHING MORE FRIGHTFUL HAS HAPPENED TO THIS ISLAND, NOTHING MORE BITTER.

Hengist and Horsa did a good job but they were greedy. They wanted lots of Vortigern's land for themselves. The Britons asked the Saxons to leave. Too late, the Saxons weren't going to budge.

Then Vortigern made an even bigger mistake. He fell in love with Hengist's daughter. Hengist said, 'You can marry her … if you give me half of your kingdom.' Vortigern said, 'Yes please!' If the Brit people argued then the Saxons just took the land anyway. Gildas wrote …

ALL THE GREAT TOWNS FELL TO THE SAXON BATTERING RAMS. BISHOPS, PRIESTS AND PEOPLE WERE ALL CHOPPED DOWN TOGETHER WHILE SWORDS FLASHED AND FLAMES CRACKLED. IT WAS HORRIBLE TO SEE THE STONES OF TOWERS THROWN DOWN TO MIX WITH PIECES OF HUMAN BODIES. BROKEN ALTARS WERE COVERED WITH A PURPLE CRUST OF CLOTTED BLOOD. THERE WAS NO BURIAL EXCEPT UNDER RUINS AND BODIES WERE EATEN BY THE BIRDS AND BEASTS.

🕷 On 24 August AD 456, Saint Bartholomew's Day, Hengist invited Vortigern to a feast. Saint Bartholomew was a Christian missionary chap who went to Armenia to preach to the pagan people. The Armenians skinned Bartholomew alive and chopped his head off. Someone should have told Vortigern, 'This is NOT a good day to meet a pagan enemy.'

🕷 Vortigern arrived at the feast with all the top lords in Britain – his best warriors, best ministers and best bishops. The savage Saxons waited till the Brits were filling their faces at the feast and then Hengist cried out, 'Saxons! Draw your knives!'

🕷 They drew great knives that they'd hidden in their boots and killed the British lords. Blood all over the tables. Blood all over the rushes on the floor. The only Briton they left alive was Vortigern. He was made a prisoner and he had to give horrible Hengist quite a lot of land just to spare his life.

There was a story that Vortigern tried to build a fortress at Dinas Emrys in North Wales. Every day it was built up – and every night it tumbled down. A wise man explained that a new building needed a blood sacrifice to the gods. That sacrifice should be the blood from a boy without a father.

Vortigern's workers found a boy with no father and his name was Merlin – the one who would grow up to be the magician in the court of King Arthur. Merlin told the builders that the wise man was not so wise after all. 'Under the ground there is a pool,' he said. 'And in the pool there are two dragons – a red dragon and a white dragon. Every night they fight, and it's their struggle that brings the tower down.'

Merlin said the red dragon was Wales and the white dragon was Saxon England. Peace would return when the red dragon defeated the white dragon. So Vortigern had to set off to defeat the Saxons. He never did, and he never got to build his fortress … but the story goes on to say King Arthur did.

The funny thing is, when archaeologists dug up the ruins of a fort at Dinas Emrys in the 1950s they really did find a deep pool.

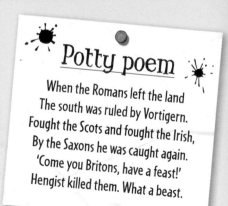

Potty poem

When the Romans left the land
The south was ruled by Vortigern.
Fought the Scots and fought the Irish,
By the Saxons he was caught again.
'Come you Britons, have a feast!'
Hengist killed them. What a beast.

16

OFFA

(757–796)

Angles and Saxons sailed across the North Sea and took over the country. There were a dozen kingdoms, small and large. Some were won with lots of blood. One of the largest kingdoms was Mercia (the English Midlands), and one of the bloodiest battlers was Offa.

Famous for ...

... the long ditch he built to mark the line between his kingdom and Wales. It is still there and is known as Offa's Dyke. The ditch is 20 m (65 ft) wide and 270 km (169 miles) long.

❀ If a Welshman was found on Offa's side of the dyke he was punished ... horribly. Offa's army would chop off the Welshman's arms.

❀ Offa ordered his lords to pay him 'food-rent'. He went around his kingdom and expected his nobles to feast and entertain him with lots of grub. How would you like the bill for 10 jars of honey, 300 loaves, 40 casks of ale, 2 oxen, 10 geese, 20 hens, 10 cheeses, a cask of butter, 5 salmon and 100 eels? And that was for just one night!

Potty poem

Offa took his throne with blood,
Liked an Offa lot of food.
Offa – bully, cruel and charmless,
Welshmen caught were left
quite armless.

18

ALFRED THE GREAT

(871–899)

In the 800s there were four great Saxon kingdoms in England – Mercia, Wessex, East Anglia and Northumbria. But the Vikings arrived and took over the north. By 878 the only Saxon kingdom left was Wessex in the south-west.

Famous for …

… leading the fight against the Vikings. Alfred's armies forced the Vikings to make peace. He said, 'You Vikings keep the North and East – you can even call it Danelaw. My Saxons will keep the South and West. We'll call it Wessex.' And they had a deal. The Viking king of the Danelaw, Guthrum, even became a Christian like Alfred.

FOUL FACTS

🌟 Saxon courts were unfair: if you had enough money you could pay the judge to let you off. King Alfred sorted out the cheating judges and replaced them with honest ones. What happened to the dishonest judges? Alfred had them hanged. They didn't do much cheating after that.

🌟 Alf was in disguise, hiding from the Vikings (they said), when he went to a poor cottage for shelter. The woman who lived there told him to look after the cakes toasting on the fire. Alfred forgot. The cakes were burned and the woman was furious. She didn't know the careless cook was her king.

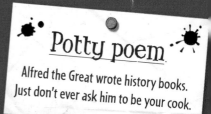

Potty poem

Alfred the Great wrote history books.
Just don't ever ask him to be your cook.

ALFRED THE GREAT
ALFRED THE GREAT? I'M ALFRED THE BLOOMIN' MARVELLOUS!
TOP 50

ATHELSTAN
(924–939)

Alf's grandson, Athelstan, took the throne 25 years after Alf died and he set about snatching back all of England from the Viking settlers.

Famous for ...

... conquering England, from Northumbria down to the south coast. He was the first king of the whole of England. Then he set about making the wild Welsh obey him.

FOUL FACTS

❋ Athelstan made sure there were strong laws and punishments. Criminals could be hanged, beheaded, stoned, drowned, burned or have their neck broken. If they weren't killed they could have bits chopped off: a hand (or two), the upper lip, nose, scalp, tongue, ear(s), eye(s) or feet.

❋ In Athelstan's day the Saxons were superstitious. For a headache they were told to take swallow chicks and cut them open, then look for little stones in their stomachs, sew them into a bag and place the bag on the head. This was also a cure for people plagued by goblins!

Potty poem

Just one king for all of England,
Tamed the Welsh too – what a man!
Granddad Alfred is remembered,
But we forget great Athelstan.
Awwww!

EDWARD THE MARTYR

(975–979)

Edward was chosen as king but his step-brother, Ethelred, was more popular.

Famous for ...

... being murdered! Elfthryth, his step-mother, had Edward killed. She wanted her own son, Ethelred, to have the crown. Edward was made a saint by the English Christians, but he was not much of a saint when he was alive – he had a terrible temper.

FOUL FACTS

❧ Edward went to Corfe Castle in the south of England to visit his step-mother and step-brother. As he climbed down from his horse he was attacked and killed by Ethelred's friends, who wanted to see Ethelred become king.

❧ When Edward was crowned, a comet appeared in the skies. Some English people thought it was a sign of bad luck. There was a terrible famine in the land so people blamed it on Edward's comet curse. When Ethelred was crowned HE had a bad-luck sign too. 'A cloud as red as blood' was seen in the sky. Unlucky for him.

Potty poem

Edward lost his temper,
Edward argued with his brother,
Edward thought it safe to meet up
With his dear step-mother.
B-i-g mistake.

EDWARD THE MARTYR

ETHELRED THE UNREADY

(979–1013 and 1014–1016)

Ethelred gained the throne by violence and he tried to keep it the same way, as new Viking raiders from Denmark started attacking.

Famous for …

… taking some really bad advice. When a new Viking army invaded, Ethelred's lords told him to give the enemy money to go away. The silver he gave them was called 'Danegeld'. Of course the Vikings came back the next year for more Danegeld … and the poor English had to keep paying out. Even after they'd been paid, the Vikings still raided and burned. They went on to murder the Archbishop of Canterbury.

FOUL FACTS

🌑 When he was a baby, Ethelred the Unready was taken to be christened. As he was held over the font, baby Ethelred peed in the holy water. The priest shook his head sadly. 'It's a sign that many English will be slaughtered,' he predicted.

🌑 Not all Vikings were hairy madmen with head-splitting axes. The Vikings who'd settled in Danelaw with families just wanted to farm. Ethelred told his army to attack the peaceful Viking villages. His troops walloped the women and even battered the babies.

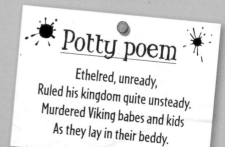

Potty poem

Ethelred, unready,
Ruled his kingdom quite unsteady.
Murdered Viking babes and kids
As they lay in their beddy.

CANUTE THE GREAT

(1016–1035)

After Ethelred died, the Viking Canute ruled over the Danelaw and the English.

Famous for …

… an episode at the seaside. Canute was a humble man. His creepy friends said he was as great as God, so Canute taught them a lesson. Canute set his throne by the sea shore. He told the tide to stop and not wet his feet and robes. A writer, Henry of Huntingdon, tells what happened:

> YET THE TIDE WENT ON RISING AS USUAL: IT DASHED OVER HIS FEET AND LEGS WITHOUT RESPECT TO HIS ROYAL PERSON. THEN THE KING LEAPT BACKWARDS, SAYING "LET ALL MEN KNOW HOW EMPTY AND WORTHLESS IS THE POWER OF KINGS."

FOUL FACTS

✹ The English rebelled. Canute fled back to Denmark, but on the way his army carved up the English prisoners and left them on the beaches to die. Canute returned and executed any English Lord who didn't support him. He even had his own son, Eadwig, killed.

✹ History books say that Alfred the Great was the only king to be called 'the Great'. They forget about Canute the Great.

Potty poem

King Canute he sat on his throne;
King Canute he had a big moan.
All the king's horses and all the kings men,
Couldn't turn waves back, not now and not then.

28

CANUTE THE GREAT

TOP
50

HAROLD II

(1066)

Just when the Vikings and the English were settling down along came a new attacker ... the Normans.

Famous for ...

... an arrow in the eye. Harold was the last Old English king. He fought William the Conqueror at the Battle of Hastings in 1066. Harold was wounded with an arrow in the eye then chopped down by Norman knights. The whole country was taken over by the Norman invaders.

FOUL FACTS

✿ King Gruffydd of Wales was on the run from Harold. Gruffydd's Welsh friends wanted peace so they killed their king before Harold could. Gruffydd's head was cut off and presented to Harold as a prezzie. Harold then married Gruffydd's widow, Edith.

✿ When Harold was hacked down at Hastings, his mum offered Harold's weight in gold for her son's body. William refused. He had it buried on the shore near Hastings. There was no gravestone to mark the spot. William wanted Harold to be forgotten.

Potty poem

Here we go, here we go, here we go,
Harold he faced a great Norman foe.
Normans fly arrows high in the sun ...
There he go, there he go, there he gone.

WILLIAM I

(1066–1087)

The Normans had arrived and they planned to stay. Anyone who rebelled was chopped like a fish-shop chip.

What's his story?

William became the last leader to conquer England when he won the Battle of Hastings. The Normans filled the country with castles. They brought in the 'Feudal System'.

Big Billy was a brutal bully and a battler. When people in the North of England rebelled he said their houses and stores of food should be burned and their animals butchered. Thousands of children, old people, young men and women died of starvation.

William was famous for his cruelty. He had a scary childhood, always in danger of being murdered by people who wanted his land. As a result he grew up tough enough to survive.

He had his first major battle in 1047, at Val-es-Dunes, at the age of just 19. Historian William of Poitiers said:

YOUNG WILLIAM WAS NOT SCARED AT THE SIGHT OF THE ENEMY SWORDS. HE HURLED HIMSELF AT HIS ENEMIES AND TERRIFIED THEM WITH SLAUGHTER. SOME OF THE ENEMY MET THEIR DEATH ON THE FIELD OF BATTLE, SOME WERE CRUSHED AND TRAMPLED IN THE RUSH TO FLEE ...

... AND MANY HORSEMEN WERE DROWNED AS THEY TRIED TO CROSS THE RIVER ORNE.

William later marched on the town of Alençon. The defenders barred its gates and then made fun of his mother's peasant family. They cried,

LEATHER! LEATHER FOR THE LEATHER-WORKER'S GRANDSON!

William was furious. When he captured the town he took 32 of the leading men of Alençon and paraded them in front of the townsfolk. He had their hands and feet cut off and probably told them to hop it.

Harold Godwinson of England was the heir to the English throne when Edward the Confessor died (which he did in 1066).

In 1064, the story goes that Harold was crossing the English Channel when his ship was caught in a storm. Harold was recognised and taken to William of Normandy (who also fancied himself as King of England). Harold had to promise he would let William become king when old King Edward died. William set him free … and Harold broke his promise. That was William's excuse for invading England in 1066.

✱ When William was crowned in London the lords all cheered. The guards outside the church thought a riot had started so they ran off in a panic and started setting fire to houses. The lords choked on smoke and ran away. Even William was shaking with fear.

✱ William died in 1087 and his body went mouldy before he could be buried. It began to turn rotten, it swelled up and smelled horrible. As the corpse was being crammed into the coffin his body burst open and bits fell off.

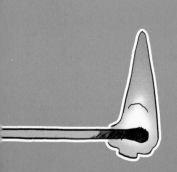

Potty poem

King Billy's a bully whose army does tricks
With arrers – them's sharp pointy sticks.
They fire them up high
'Watch me eye!' Harold cries,
At Hastings in ten-sixty-six.

WILLIAM II

(1087–1100)

The Conqueror's son was known as 'Rufus' because that was the Roman word for 'red' and Willy Two had red hair and a red face.

Famous for ...

... a hunting accident in the New Forest. A hunter fired an arrow at a deer, missed the animal but hit the king and killed him.

FOUL FACTS

🟤 William and his brother Henry hated one another. Henry was out hunting in the same forest on the same day as William when the king was shot. Did Henry fire the deadly arrow? It's a history mystery.

🟤 The dead king's body was dumped on a cart and taken to Winchester Cathedral. He was buried under the tower of the cathedral. Seven years later the tower fell down ... William's ghost got the blame.

OH DEAR!

Potty poem

William Two is a rotten old king,
With a face so tomatoey red.
He shoots little deer, so it serves Billy right
When he cops a sharp arrow instead!

HENRY I

(1100–1135)

The Conqueror's younger son, Henry, was just as cruel as his deadly dad.

Famous for ...

... being a strong king who made laws that were fair. He was a tough man yet he was terrified of being murdered. The idea of assassins gave him nightmares.

FOUL FACTS

🟥 Henry had a strong sense of loyalty. In 1090 a man made a promise to Henry's brother (and greatest enemy) Robert. The man broke that promise. You would think Henry might reward the man. Henry pushed the man off the top of Rouen Castle. Splat! In future Henry's followers took their promises seriously. Very seriously.

🟥 Henry's doctor warned him not to eat too much rich food, but the king loved a fish called a lamprey – an eel. He stuffed his face with lampreys and it killed him ... just like the doctor said it would.

Potty poem

The chief defect of Henry (King)
Was eating lampreys (fish like string).
When he ate one plate (too many)
It was bye-bye to King (Henry).

HENRY I

50

STEPHEN (1135–1154)
& MATILDA (1141)

Henry had left his lands in France to his nephew, Stephen. He left the English throne to his daughter, Matilda, but Stephen wanted both and went to war with Matilda.

Famous for …

… wars that made England a miserable place to live.

FOUL FACTS

✷ In 1141, Matilda was trapped by Stephen's army in Devizes town. She dressed up in grave clothes and was put in a coffin where she pretended to be dead. She was carried out like a corpse and escaped.

✷ That same year, Matilda was trapped in Oxford on a snowy winter night. Stephen's soldiers were all around. When the food ran out she put on a large white cloak and escaped over the wall. The white cloak hid her in the snow.

Potty poem

There once was a queen called Matilda
Who escaped through the snow –
bet that chilled 'er.
Her enemy, Stephen,
Was keen to get even.
If he'd caught her he'd surely
have killed 'er.

STEPHEN & MATILDA

TOP
50

HENRY II

(1154–1189)

Henry spent a lot of his time going to war with his three sons AND his wife Eleanor.

Famous for ...

... a murder in Canterbury Cathedral. Henry made his friend, Thomas Becket, head of the church in England. Then they argued and Henry said he wanted rid of Thomas. Four knights thought he meant he wanted him killed ... they rode off to Canterbury and murdered Thomas at his altar. The knights attacked Thomas when he had no sword. They hit him so hard on the skull his brains spilled out onto the cathedral floor.

FOUL FACTS

🌑 When Henry II died his body was carried to the grave in an open coffin. His hated son, Richard I, arrived to look at the body. Richard leaned over the coffin and blood spurted from the nose of his dead father. 'His angry ghost doesn't want his son there!' people muttered.

Potty poem

'I am sorry,' said old Henry, 'That my old pal Tom is dead.
You knights were really silly to go bashing in his head.
'Cos Tom was quite a nice guy. If you had to take a life,
You could have had a chop or four at my three sons and my wife!'

HENRY II

TOP 50

TOP 10: WOEFUL WELSH RULERS

The Welsh had their own kings until the Normans invaded. Then their lands were taken over by the mighty Norman barons.

1. CARATACUS
(DIED AROUND AD 50)

When the Romans invaded in AD 48 this warrior stirred up the Silures tribe down in South Wales. Caratacus was one of the first ever Welsh heroes. He attacked Roman supplies and robbed them. He also attacked tribes (like the Dubonni) who wanted to be friends with the Romans. The Roman writer Tacitus said:

THE SILURES, A FIERCE PEOPLE, WERE NOW BRAVE IN THE MIGHT OF CARATACUS – BY MANY BATTLES HE HAD RAISED HIMSELF FAR ABOVE ALL THE OTHER GENERALS OF THE BRITONS.

But by AD 75 the Romans ruled Wales and the country needed a new warrior-king.

44

2. CADWALLON AP EINION
(LIVED 460–534)

This Welsh warrior reigned from around the year 500. His nickname was Cadwallon 'Long Hand'. He drove the Irish out of North Wales where they had invaded. He may have been called 'Long Hand' because he had really long arms. A Welsh poet wrote:

CADWALLON AP CADFAN

CADWALLON 'LONG HAND' COULD REACH A STONE FROM THE GROUND TO KILL A RAVEN, WITHOUT BENDING HIS BACK, BECAUSE HIS ARM WAS AS LONG AS HIS SIDE TO THE GROUND.

3. CADWALLON AP CADFAN
(625–634)

In 616 the Saxon King Ethelfrith attacked Chester and 1,200 Welsh monks were murdered. King Cadwallon of Gwyneth took the Welsh fight to the Saxon lands. Cadwallon won a battle near Doncaster, killing King Edwin of Northumbria and lopping off his head. Cadwallon also killed off the young English princes and took over Northumbria. He wasn't a very nice man. The historian monk Bede wrote …

AT THIS TIME THERE WAS A GREAT SLAUGHTER BOTH OF THE CHURCH AND OF THE PEOPLE OF NORTHUMBRIA. THE BARBARIAN CADWALLON WAS A CHRISTIAN BY NAME BUT A SAVAGE AT HEART AND SPARED NEITHER WOMEN NOR CHILDREN. WITH BEASTLY CRUELTY HE PUT ALL TO DEATH BY TORTURE AND FOR A LONG TIME RAGED THROUGH ALL THEIR LAND, MEANING TO WIPE OUT THE WHOLE OF THE ENGLISH NATION FROM THE LAND OF BRITAIN.

But Cadwallon only ruled a year before getting himself killed at a battle near Hexham, Northumberland, in 635.

4. RHODRI MAWR
(844–878)

The Vikings were sailing along the coast of Wales in 850 and doing pillages of villages. Rhodri led the fight-back … until he died fighting the English.

RHODRI MAWR

5. HYWEL DDA (942–950)

In the year 927 the Welsh princes agreed to be ruled by the English king. But there were still some great Welsh princes. There were people like Hywel Dda (meaning 'the Good'). Of course he wasn't all THAT good – he had his brother-in-law killed. But Hywel did create the 'Laws of Hywel' that would be in force in Wales for hundreds of years. They were sensible laws which had less of the old 'punishment' and more 'pay for your crime'. Hywel's laws saw women as almost equal to men. Almost – but not quite. If you killed a slave you'd have to pay his master one oxen. But if it was a woman slave it would only cost you half an oxen. Not so 'Good' Hywel.

6. GRUFFYDD AP LLYWELYN (1055–1063)

Gruffydd was last Welsh 'high king'. By 1057 he had battled and murdered his way to all the thrones of Wales. He was jealous of his wife, Edith. He once heard that a young man dreamed about cuddling Edith and he wanted the young man tortured to death. But in 1063 Gruffydd was beaten by Harold Godwinson (who later became Harold II of England) and then assassinated ... probably by his own men.

7. OWAIN AP GRUFFYDD (1137–1170)

By 1152 Owain ap Gruffydd had made himself a powerful leader of Wales. He wasn't too bothered who he hurt to get there. He took his cousin, Cunedda ap Cadwallon, ripped out his eyes and cut off his naughty bits. When awful Owain died, the horror wasn't over. The Archbishop of Canterbury decided to turn up at the funeral and told the priests Owain should not be buried in the church – he was so evil he should be dumped in a field.

8. LLYWELYN THE GREAT (1200–1240)

LLYWELYN THE GREAT

Llywelyn married English King John's daughter, Joan, in 1205 but that didn't stop him going to war with John in 1211. At first King John suffered. Llywelyn burned English castles. A monk wrote …

AND KING JOHN CAME AS FAR AS CHESTER. AND THERE HIS ARMY SUFFERED SUCH A LACK OF FOOD THAT AN EGG WAS SOLD FOR A PENNY–HALFPENNY, AND THEY FOUND THE FLESH OF THEIR HORSES AS GOOD AS THE BEST DISHES.

THEN Llywelyn plotted with the French to invade England. King John took a terrible revenge. He was holding 28 Welsh boys as hostages. He hanged them all from the walls of his castle.

9. LLYWELYN AP GRUFFYDD (1256–1277)

Edward I became King of England and set about turning England into 'Britain'. He hated Llywelyn and battered the Welsh. He even had Llywelyn's bride, Eleanor, kidnapped on the way to her wedding. Llywelyn burned English castles in revenge and went off to gather a new army. While he was gone, the old army was attacked and surrendered. The Welsh laid down their weapons ... and the English slaughtered them.

10. OWAIN GLYNDWR (LEADER OF THE WELSH 1400–1412)

Owain Glyndwr was one of the richest of the Welsh nobles. The peasants elected him as their leader to rebel against their English lords. The rebellion failed and the Welsh were worse off than ever. But the poor peasants never forgot him. In the 1700s the Welsh writer, Thomas Pennant, collected the stories of Owain that praised him as the chief hero of the Welsh. Legends say that he's still alive – sitting in a cave playing chess with King Arthur. Waiting for the day when the Welsh need a hero to save them.

OWAIN GLYNDWR

49

RICHARD I
(1189–1199)

Henry II's rebel son, Richard I, took the throne when his father died.

Famous for …

… crusading. This famous warrior king was known as 'Lionheart'. He spent so much time fighting in Palestine in the Crusades that he spent less than a year of his reign in England. He was captured by his enemy and the English people had to pay a huge ransom to set him free.

FOUL FACTS

✿ Richard once hid from his enemies in a kitchen. He forgot to take off his royal ring so they spotted him and locked him up.

✿ One historian said that Richard kept a supply of prisoners with his army. If his soldiers ran out of food, they could always eat them. That may not be true. But he did take enemy prisoners at the siege of Acre in the Holy Land – and then gave the order to slaughter them all.

✿ During the siege of a French castle Richard died from a poisoned arrow in the neck.

Potty poem

Richard, strong and lion-hearted,
Was from England often parted.
Spent his life in places sunny.
Still the English gave the money
To release him. Ain't life funny?

JOHN
(1199–1216)

John, Richard I's younger brother, was delighted when Lionheart died and he could take over.

Famous for ...

... being hated! He was supposed to be the worst king England ever had. Legend says he wanted to steal the crown from Richard, and that he fought against Robin Hood to keep it. His angry barons made him sign a promise to give power to the people – this deed is known as the Magna Carta.

FOUL FACTS

🐾 John captured his problem nephew, Arthur. He got drunk one night in Paris, killed Arthur, tied a stone round his body and threw the corpse in the River Seine.

🐾 John once tried to cross a stretch of muddy sand called the Wash. He began the crossing but the tide rushed in. He escaped with his life but lost his crown and chests of jewels.

Potty poem

First John, last John,
John One, only one,
Never had another John.
John One, only one,
Cos of all the things he done,
John One, only one.

TOP
50

HENRY III

(1216–1272)

English kings still thought they should rule France too, just as William the Conqueror had done. Henry raised a lot of taxes for wars against France. It was all wasted because he lost.

Famous for ...

... a l-o-n-g reign. He ruled for 56 years, one of the longest reigns of any English king. He called a Great Council which was the first parliament of the people.

FOUL FACTS

🌸 Henry went to war with the English barons, who were led by Simon de Montfort. Henry's supporters fought Simon at the Battle of Evesham. He was killed with a lance in the throat then chopped to pieces. The killer sent Simon's head to his own wife to show off.

🌸 Henry III sent his queen, Eleanor, to the Tower of London. She was there because the people hated her and the Tower was a safe shelter. Henry kept a zoo there with a camel, a buffalo, a lion, an elephant and leopards ... and his wife! When she went out on the River Thames the Londoners pelted her with rubbish. She threw it back.

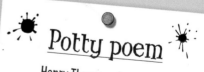

Potty poem

Henry Three was just as bad
As the last king (John), his dad.
John, at least, did not last long,
But Henry Three went on and on and on
and on and on and on ...

EDWARD I
(1272–1307)

After falling out with Dad, Henry III, during the baron's rebellion, Edward made up with his pa and took over the crown.

What's his story?

Edward was a warrior who fought the French, the Scots and the Welsh. He made his baby son the 'Prince of Wales'. (The ruler's oldest son is still given that name today.) This was to stop any Welsh lord ever ruling in Wales again.

Edward I was even more famous for battling and beating the Scots.

Just like his dad, he said he was king of France and went to war to prove it. These wars all cost a lot of money, which meant a lot of taxes for the English peasants.

FOUL FACTS

Edward enjoyed a good battle...

✸ He set off on a Crusade in the Middle East with a little army of just 1,000 men. He was stabbed by an enemy assassin with a poisoned dagger and almost died.

❃ Edward returned to England and in 1282 decided to crush rebels in Wales led by Llywelyn ap Gruffydd.

❃ Llywelyn's head was cut off in a battle and shown to the English troops. Edward sent the head to London. In London it was set up in the city pillory (like the stocks) for a day and crowned with ivy (to show that Llywelyn was a 'king' of outlaws).

❃ Then the head was carried by a horseman on the point of his lance to the Tower of London and set up over the gate. It was still on the Tower of London 15 years later.

❃ Llywelyn's brother, Dafydd, was killed by being hanged, drawn and quartered. He was the first important man to suffer that terrible death – but not the last.

❃ In 1296 Edward invaded Scotland. The English captured the Scottish leader, William Wallace, in 1305 and he too was hanged, drawn and quartered.

❃ Edward set off to batter the new Scottish king, Robert the Bruce, but he died on the journey.

❃ A wool merchant called Richard de Podlicote dug a tunnel under Westminster Abbey and stole Edward's crown jewels. About 50 mischievous monks helped. But they were caught. Richard was hanged and his skin was stretched across the treasure-house door. It was a warning to anyone else who fancied thieving from Ed.

❃ There is a legend that says Edward had Welsh poets burned because he was at war with Wales. It isn't true. He did set fire to Welsh poetry books though.

* Another fake story said that King Edward came to Caernarfon Castle to have his baby son crowned Prince of Wales. It was said that ...

* Edward I's wife gave birth to a son, Edward II, at Caernarfon Castle. The king called the baby 'Prince of Wales and Count of Chester'. It was meant to make the Wild Welsh happy to have their own prince.

* The legend says that in 1300 Edward I went to Caernarfon and said to the people of Wales, 'Here is my eldest son.' He then raised the baby above his head. He told the Welsh people 'Behold! I give you a prince born in Wales who could speak never a word of English.' But the truth is ... he'd have had a job to hold his son above his head – the prince was 16 years old by then! And anyway young Prince Edward himself spoke French.

* The story ends by saying the child grew up to be King Edward II and he was the first English Prince of Wales. But the truth is ... he was given the Prince of Wales title in Lincoln, not Caernarfon. Caernarfon Castle wasn't finished till 1330. In 1301 Edward would have been standing on a building site.

* As Edward lay dying in 1307 he asked for his bones to be taken into the battle against the Scots for luck. After all, he was known as 'The Hammer of the Scots'. His wishes were not carried out. He was buried.

Potty poem

Edward hated every Scot;
Went to fight them quite a lot.
Dying, he said, 'Tell you what,
Put my body in a pot;
Boil it up so nice and hot;
Take my bones out, they won't rot,
Won't go mouldy, turn to grot.
Every time you fight the Scot,
Take me with you, fail me not.'

58

EDWARD II

(1307–1327)

When Edward I died young, Edward II lost the Scottish battles his father had won.

Famous for …

… a woeful wife! He married Queen Isabella of France. When her son, Edward III, was born she wanted rid of her husband so her child could take over. Her friends captured the king and threw him into a castle prison.

FOUL FACTS

✤ The corpses of dead prisoners were left to rot under Edward's cell. Isabella hoped Ed would die from an infection. He didn't. There is a savage story that his jailers pushed a red hot poker up his bottom to finish him off.

✤ Isabella may have had Edward murdered, yet she was buried with his heart clutched to her chest – a sign of true love. A poet called her 'The She-Wolf of France'.

Potty poem

'Careful what you're doing with that poker,'
Edward said.
(The wicked soldiers' eyes were like the poker – glowing red.)
'You want me to lie down here? I ain't tired.
Here – stop pushin'!'
(The wicked soldiers held him down and smothered him with cushions.)
'Nng-nng-nng-nng! Nng-nng-nng-nng!'
poor old Edward cried.
Till they stuck the poker in him. Then he said no more. He'd died.

EDWARD II

EDWARD III

(1327–1377)

Isabella got her way and her son Edward took the throne when he was just 14.

Famous for ...

... starting the Hundred Years' War. Little Edward III decided he was King of France as well as England (yes, another one) and that started a long war against the French. He won great battles at Crécy and Poitiers thanks to the power of English and Welsh archers.

Potty poem

Edward Three was always off to war with
Scots and French and others.
Called himself the 'King of France' and
that caused lots of bother.
Fought the French at Poitiers, then again
at Crécy.
English arrows filled the air ... the end
was rather messy.

FOUL FACTS

✸ Edward III was king when the Black Death came to Britain. A writer said ...

> 'THERE APPEARED CERTAIN SWELLINGS IN THE GROIN AND UNDER THE ARMPIT, THE VICTIMS SPAT BLOOD, AND IN THREE DAYS THEY WERE DEAD.'

These swellings oozed with blood and pus. Purple-black blotches appeared on the skin and you smelled really horrible.

✸ Edward III's teacher said that he ruined books by letting his nose dribble over the pages. He would eat fruit and cheese or drink while reading, allowing it to slop on to the pages. He also had filthy fingernails.

RICHARD II

(1377–1399)

Edward III reigned for over 50 years and his son, the Black Prince, died before him. The crown went to Edward's grandson, Richard, aged ten.

Famous for …

… putting a stop to the Peasants' Revolt. The poor people hated a new tax called the Poll Tax and their revolt was led by Wat Tyler. Tyler and Richard met in a field near London to talk about peace. Tyler was hacked to death by the Mayor of London. End of revolt.

FOUL FACTS

✹ Richard was such a rotten ruler that his cousin, Henry IV, threw him off the throne. Richard was locked away in Pontefract Castle. He was so miserable he seemed to lose the will to live. He probably starved himself to death.

✹ Richard's first wife, Anne, died from the plague. He took a second wife, Isabella of France, when she was aged just six. It brought a little peace in the Hundred Years' War. When Richard was dead she went home, married again, then died at the age of 19. What a life!

Potty poem

Tyler led the peasant mob, cried,
'I'm the leader, I'm the biz!'
Richard Two said, 'What's your name?'
Tyler said, 'That's right, it is!'

HENRY IV

(1399–1413)

Richard II was a weak king so his cousin, Henry, took his throne. Henry IV never enjoyed being king.

Famous for ...

... so much bad luck that people thought he was cursed. Henry IV had so many lice in his hair it was said that his hair wouldn't grow on his itchy scalp. He was said to suffer from leprosy; his spotty skin itched; and his eyes were dry, red and sore.

FOUL FACTS

🌸 Henry IV had only been on the throne three months when some of Richard II's supporters led a rebellion against him. The leaders were not only executed, but had their corpses cut into pieces and carted off to London in sacks.

🌸 Stories said the curse of Henry spread across England. Evil signs were:
* a boy born with one eye in the middle of his forehead
* a calf born with two tails
* eggs which, when cooked and opened, showed the face of a man with white hair.

Potty poem

Nobody likes me, 'specially them Scots
(Me skin is all mouldy and covered in spots).
Even my own son is not very nice
(Me head is so itchy because of the lice).
Kingdom and crown, they are worth simply nothin'
(Me eyes are as dry as the dust in a coffin).
Nightmares each night and no hair on me head;
To tell you the truth, I'd be better off dead.

66

TOP 10: IREFUL IRISH RULERS

Ireland had a lot of battles with Britain over who ruled the Irish. For a long time though, they had their own kings.

1. TIGERNMAS
(1621–1544 BC)

Tigernmas killed his cousin to become King of Ireland. The Irish started mining gold and silver during his reign. He also brought in the wearing of coloured clothing ... tartan. The name Tigernmas means 'Lord of Death'. Tigernmas liked nothing better than a bit of human sacrifice at Halloween, when children were chopped. Blood all over the place. The followers of Tigernmas got a bit carried away one horrific Halloween and killed him. No surprise there.

TIGERNMAS

3. EOCHAID FEIDLECH
(94–82 BC)

2. LABRAID LOINGSECH
LIVED 268 BC)

King Eochaid's wife and three sons went to war against him (the same thing happened to Henry II of England many years later). Eochaid Feidlech killed his rebel sons and cut off their heads. It broke his heart and he died.

Labraid's father was high king but was murdered by his brother, Cobhthatch. The evil Uncle Cobhthatch forced Labraid to eat a piece of his father's heart AND a mouse. The shock turned Labraid dumb for many years. When he was old enough he raised an army, trapped Cobhthatch in a hall and burned it to the ground. Revenge.

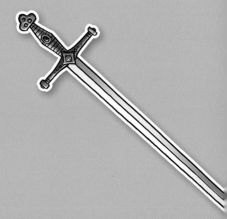

69

4. MAEVE
(LIVED SOMETIME BETWEEN 50 BC AND AD 50)

MAEVE

Maeve was the daughter of Eochaid Feidlech and queen of Connacht. She murdered her sister. Years later the dead sister's son, Furbaide, took his revenge. Maeve used to swim in a lake. Furbaide practised with his sling and the next time he saw his Aunt Maeve bathing, he killed her with a piece of cheese. From cheddar to deader.

5. ÁED RÓIN
(708–735)

By the 700s Ireland was a Christian country but that didn't make for peace. Áed Róin was a king of Ulster (Northern Ireland) when he upset the Abbot of Armagh. The Abbot told his followers he wanted revenge. What he got was Áed Róin's head.

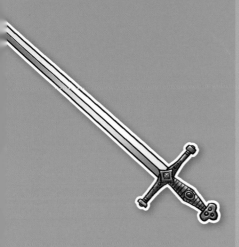

In 1014 it was said that blood rained from the sky, and that soldiers were attacked by spears that flew out of walls and by ravens with iron beaks. In an Irish battle against the Vikings at Clontarf, the Irish king, Brian Boru, won and knelt down to pray and thank God. As he was kneeling he was chopped by his Viking enemy.

6. MÁEL SECHNAILL
(846–862)

The Vikings started raiding Ireland in the 800s and the Irish kings struggled to defend their lands. Máel became king of 'Mide' (Middle Ireland) in the usual way … he killed his brother, Flann. He took over 'Tara' (East Ireland) when the old king drowned. Máel went on to kill his cousin, but his main battles were against the Vikings.

BRIAN BORU

8. STRONGBOW
(1170–1176)

William the Conqueror conquered England in 1066 but it was another hundred years before the nasty Normans got around to battering the Irish. 'Strongbow' was the nickname of the Norman Richard, Earl of Pembroke. The king of Leinster (Dermott MacMurrough) invited Strongbow to come to Ireland to sort out his old enemy, Rory O'Connor. Naturally Strongbow ended up taking over a large part of Ireland. Never trust a Norman. King Dermott MacMurrough was cursed, the Irish said, and his punishment for inviting Strongbow was that he rotted to death. In 1170 Strongbow's army landed in Waterford. They didn't simply execute 70 Waterford leaders … they took them to Baginbun Head, chopped off their arms, legs and heads, and threw the bits into the creek. Ireland wouldn't be free of English control again till 1922.

9. SHANE O'NEILL
(1559–1567)

Shane was a king in Ulster who rebelled against Elizabeth I's rule. He was known as Shane the Proud and was a ruthless ruler. When a servant was late serving his dinner he had the man's ears cut off. Shane was defeated in battle by an old enemy, the O'Donnell family. He surrendered and was taken prisoner. The O'Donnells beheaded him and sent his head to the English rulers in Dublin. Elizabeth I was a happy queen to be rid of the rebel.

72

10. GRACE O'MALLEY
(LIVED 1530–1603)

Grace was born into a family of Irish sailors and landowners. She married the vicious Donal O'Flaherty – it was said he murdered his sister's step-son when he thought the boy was getting too much power. In 1593 her sons were arrested as rebels so Grace went to London to ask Queen Elizabeth I for their release. The two women were nearly the same age (about 60) when they met at Greenwich Palace. Grace wore a fine gown, but she had a hidden dagger. Guards found it before she could attack the queen. Grace said she only had the dagger to defend herself. Queen Elizabeth believed her.

GRACE O'MALLEY

HENRY V
(1413–1422)

Henry took over from his dead dad. They had argued so it wasn't a sad-Dad day. Henry V also took over the Hundred Years' War against France.

Famous for ...

... his bravery in battle. The Shakespeare play shows Henry V as a wild young man who calmed down and became a great warrior. He saw a gap in the enemy walls (a 'breach') and led from the front crying,

'ONCE MORE UNTO THE BREACH DEAR FRIENDS, OR FILL THE WALL UP WITH OUR ENGLISH DEAD.'

FOUL FACTS

🌸 At the brutal battle of Agincourt the English took a lot of French prisoners. When there was a fresh French attack, Henry was worried that the prisoners would join in and attack him from the back. He ordered that all the French prisoners should be murdered.

🌸 The French king decided to make fun of Henry. He sent the young English king a present. Tennis balls. He was saying, 'You'd be better off playing tennis than trying to make war against France.' Henry crossed the channel and his small army beat the large French army.

Potty poem

As Henry rode to fight the French,
He cried, 'Once more unto the breach!
But put that spade and bucket down
You fool! No! I did not say beach!'

74

HENRY VI

(1422–1461 and 1470–1471)

Henry V died of disease and the crown passed to his feeble little son, Henry VI, aged eight months.

What's his story?

… young Henry VI was so weak the great families of England went to war over his throne. Henry's family, the Lancasters, wore the sign of a red rose. His enemies, the Yorks, wore a white rose. They fought each other in 30 years of bitter wars known as the 'Wars of the Roses'.

Henry VI was king when England finally lost the Hundred Years' War against France. It was a great blow to England when the French found a great warrior leader, Joan of Arc, in 1429.

✸ Joan of Arc was a peasant shepherd when she heard an angel's voice telling her to become a soldier, drive the English out and put Prince Louis back on the throne of France.

✸ She led the French to some great victories until she was captured and handed over to the English. They wanted her dead, but you aren't supposed to kill a prisoner of war.

✸ She was handed over to a bishop who put her on trial.

✸ Joan was found guilty of being a witch. As punishment she was tied to a wooden stake on top of a pile of wood. It was set on fire and she was burned alive. She was only about 19 years old.

🐾 After losing the wars in France, the English started fighting against one another.

When the Yorks fought Henry VI's Lancasters at the Battle of Towton (in Yorkshire) in 1461 the commanders said, 'Take no prisoners. Kill them all.' It became the bloodiest battle ever fought in Britain.

King Henry VI lost that battle and was later captured and taken to the Tower of London. He died there ... maybe murdered by Yorkist leader Richard.

FOUL FACTS

🌸 Henry VI had the job of opening Parliament. He was taken to Westminster but sat and cried all the way through the ceremony. You can't blame him. He was only three years old at the time.

🌸 Henry VI had been a weak king because he was often ill. From August 1453 until Christmas 1454, Henry ...

● sat still and silent for hours like a statue

● lost his memory

● didn't recognise anyone

● found it difficult to move without help

● didn't know his wife had given birth to their son. When he recovered his memory Queen Margaret was able to tell him he had a new son, the baby Prince Edward.

Potty poem

Henry was a gentle monarch,
Soft and fragile, like a flower,
Or the Roses that were fought for;
Till they 'pruned' him in the Tower.

HENRY VI

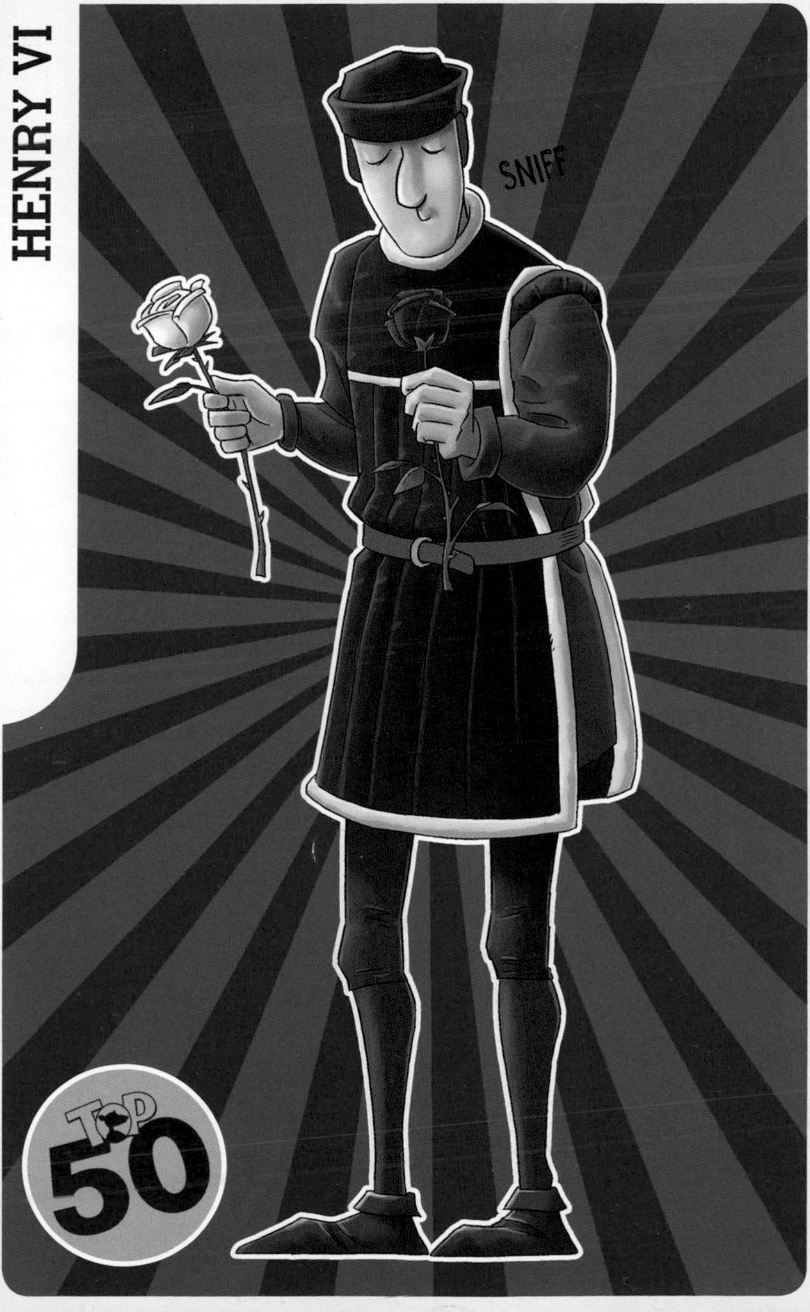

EDWARD IV

1461–1483

The Yorks were winning the Wars of the Roses so top Yorkist, Edward IV, took the throne.

Famous for …

… marrying the enemy! Edward won the Wars of the Roses … for a while. Then the tall and handsome Ed married Elizabeth from the Red Rose Lancaster family. Edward didn't care who he had upset. He was king now and thought he could do anything he liked. A lot of Edward's old friends – the White Rose fighters – were very unhappy and they started the war all over again.

FOUL FACTS

✿ He had two brothers, the loyal Richard and the wicked George. When George plotted against him, Edward IV had George executed. They say George was drowned in a barrel of wine. (But the traitor didn't whine about it.)

✿ At the Battle of Barnet in 1471 one side fought under a flag with a star on it. The other side fought under the sign of a flaming sun. Friends of the star army attacked their own side because they mistook the star for a sun. They lost the battle. Not surprising.

Potty poem

'Oooh! I'm handsome, ooh, I'm great.
(Pass the wine and pass the plate.)
Ooh, I love food, wine and wealth …
But, most of all, I love myself.'

EDWARD IV

TOP 50

EDWARD V

1483

Edward IV died quite young and his son, Edward V, was only 12 when he became king ... for a few weeks.

Famous for ...

... having a wicked uncle. Edward V's Uncle Richard said Edward was too young to run the country. He said HE would run England till Edward was old enough. Edward and his younger brother were put in the Tower of London, so they would be 'safe' from enemies.

FOUL FACTS

🌑 Edward V was never seen again. A historian, Thomas More, said the two boys were murdered on the orders of Uncle Richard.

🌑 In 1674 workmen repairing a staircase at the foot of the White Tower (the Tower of London's keep) came across two skeletons. They were the remains of two children aged 10 and 12 ... just the ages the princes would have been if they had died in the reign of Richard, their uncle. So did Richard have them smothered in their beds and snatch Ed's crown? That's what an old story says.

Potty poem

Take a young lad, and give him a crown,
Take a young lad without any cares.
Take a young lad and bury him down,
Deep in a tower and under the stairs.

EDWARD V

RICHARD III

(1483–1485)

Richard said he would rule until Edward was old enough to be king. Then, after a couple of months, he got the lords to agree HE should be the next king, Richard III.

What's his story?

A hundred years after Richard III died, William Shakespeare wrote a play about him. In the play he was shown as an evil, monstrous man. He was born with all his teeth and hair, Shakespeare said. He grew up with a hunched back. He had the Princes in the Tower murdered and became the cruellest king England had ever seen.

Shakespeare's play ends when Richard fights his last battle at Bosworth Field. As his enemies close in on him he sees there is no escape. In the play Richard cries out, 'A horse, a horse. My kingdom for a horse.' But the horse never came and Richard was hacked down.

The truth is, no one is really sure what happened to the Princes in the Tower. Richard was quite a good king for two years. In his final battle historians said he died crying out against his enemies, 'Treason, treason!' He didn't die shouting for a horse – Shakespeare invented that.

❈ England was invaded by the last Lancaster, Henry Tudor. He landed in Wales and marched an army into England to meet Richard in battle. Richard sat with his army on the top of Ambien Hill near Bosworth. As the battle turned against Richard's army, the king decided to charge down the hill and risk his own life.

❈ Richard led the charge and fought bravely. Henry Tudor's flag-carrier held up the Tudor flag. Richard chopped off his arm. He almost reached Henry Tudor before he was hauled off his horse and killed.

❈ Richard III had some traitors among his army. Sir Thomas Stanley couldn't be trusted in the battle. (The invader, Henry Tudor, was Sir Thomas's step-son.) So Richard snatched Thomas's younger son as a hostage. 'Make sure you fight with me or the boy will be executed,' the king said. Sir Thomas shrugged and said, 'I have other sons.'

Richard lost the battle because Sir Thomas refused to help him. Did Richard's followers kill the boy? Of course not! They saw Richard III defeated and knew that murdering one of the winner's family would be a bad move.

 It is said that treacherous Thomas Stanley found Richard's crown on a thorn bush and placed it on step-son Henry Tudor's head. Henry repaid him years later – by executing his brother, William Stanley!

 Richard's body was stripped and dragged off to be buried in a forgotten grave in Leicester. In 2012 it was discovered again and dug up. It had been found under a car park.

Potty poem

Richard Three was like a villain in a pantomime;
Limping round and cackling at his latest evil crime;
Went around dark castles trying to murder little kids.
Oh no he didn't!
Oh yes he did!

Richard Three was born with all his hair and all his teeth;
Wicked little eyes on top and twisted legs beneath.
Had the little princes smothered and their bodies hidden.
Oh yes he did!
Oh no he didn't!

Richard had a twisted face, a hunch upon his back,
Forced the poor Anne to marry him, alas and alack!
He's the sort of monster in the darkness always lurking.
Look out! He's be-hind you!
No he isn't!
Are you cer-tain?

HENRY VII

(1485–1509)

Henry Tudor brought a new and wonderful gift to the English people. Peace. The Red Rose Lancaster king married Elizabeth, daughter of White Rose Edward IV. The Wars of the Roses were finally over.

Famous for ...

... being stingy! The first of the Terrible Tudors wasn't as vicious as his son, Henry VIII, or his grandchildren, Mary and Elizabeth I, but he was very mean with money. The gossips in the palace said his queen wore buckles of tin on her shoes because the King was too mean to buy her silver. Her gowns were mended time and time again, frayed cuffs turned up and worn threads patched.

FOUL FACTS

❀ There were at least TEN people with a better claim to the throne of England than Henry Tudor. One of them was his own mother. A boy called Lambert Simnel said he was one of the Princes in the Tower and wanted his throne back. Henry defeated Lambert's rebellion and gave him a job as a kitchen boy.

❀ Henry VII had a pet monkey. There is a story that the monkey got into Henry's writing room and tore up his diaries. Since the diaries had nasty notes about the people in Henry's court, it is possible that one of them let the monkey in – and had a good laugh.

Potty poem

H is for Henry the Tudor who wed
E for Elizabeth (daughter of Ed).
N is for no-one could
R for rebel.
Y is it so hard to like Henry well?

HENRY VIII
(1509–1547)

Henry VII died and the terrible Tudor, Henry VIII, took his place.

Famous for ...

... having six wives. What's more, he was clearly never satisfied. He divorced two, beheaded two and one died. The last one lived on after he died.

FOUL FACTS

✹ Henry VIII had hunting hounds who ate scraps the king threw from the table. But after he died, and was lying in his coffin, some attendants said the hounds were looking lovingly at the body ... and licking their lips. The rotting body started to ooze and foul juices dribbled out. The hounds lapped it up.

✹ Henry VIII was a Catholic but the Pope refused to let him marry wife number two, Anne. So Henry changed to become a Protestant ... he created the Church of England, made himself top man, and told himself he could marry Anne. He executed Catholics and he closed down monasteries and threw out the monks.

✹ But Henry's daughter, Mary, was a Catholic. There is a story that when Mary came to the throne she had Henry's bones dug up. She said her father was one of those wicked Protestants – so she had his body burned.

Potty poem

Henry eight – wives six.
(Seems to chop them up like sticks.)
Daughters two – sons one.
(No grandchildren. Tudors gone.)
Henry ate – Monks nil.
(All that eating made him ill.)
Thomas More – Henry no more.
(Death just evened up the score.)

EDWARD VI

(1547–1553)

Henry died and his young son, Edward, became king at the age of nine.

Famous for ...

... being poorly all the time. Edward VI was the son of Henry VIII's third wife, Jane Seymour. She died soon after he was born, and he was sick for all of his short life. He was a religious child who liked the Church of England so much he had a new Prayer Book written.

Potty poem

What can be said
About poor Ed?
Mother died in his birth bed.
Cut off uncle Seymour's head.
Books and prayers were all well read.
Never loved and never wed.
Got to fifteen then dropped dead.

FOUL FACTS

✤ Edward died of a lung disease, tuberculosis, at the age of 15. This had one or two nasty side effects:

> 'ERUPTIONS CAME OUT OVER HIS SKIN, HIS HAIR FELL OFF, AND THEN HIS NAILS, AND AFTERWARDS THE JOINTS OF HIS TOES AND FINGERS.'

✤ Edward VI wrote poetry; not very cheerful poetry. It included this moan about being a monarch ...

> 'KINGDOMS ARE BUT CARES.'

He was King of England but miserable about it. Silly boy.

MARY I

(1553–1558)

When Edward died his older half-sister, Mary, took the throne. She tried to turn the country back to being Catholic. was just 16 years old. Mary also thought about having her half-sister, Elizabeth, beheaded and locked her away for many months.

Famous for ...

... burning lots of people at the stake. Mary wanted everyone to be Catholic. If they refused they were burned alive. In a few years 300 English people were set alight, dying slowly and horribly. A writer gave her the name that stuck: Bloody Mary.

🌸 Mary married Philip, the king of Spain. But Philip was a pretty awful choice and he never liked her much. He left Mary soon after their marriage. He went to fight the French and broke Mary's heart. She tried to get him to come back by sending him his favourite food – her meat pies.

FOUL FACTS

🌸 Edward VI said he wanted his Protestant cousin, Lady Jane Grey, to have the throne after he died. Mary had Jane Grey arrested and beheaded. Jane

Potty poem

Catholic Mary is quite scary
When it comes to Prot-e-stants.
Sticks them on a great big bonfire
Till they singe their underpants!

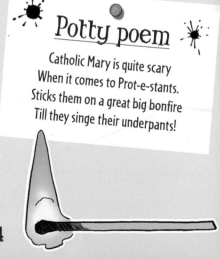

94

MARY I

TOP 50

ELIZABETH I

(1558–1603)

From Mary the crown passed to Elizabeth – and back to the Protestants.

What's her story?

Elizabeth made the Catholics pay for their burning of Protestants. It was the Catholics' turn to be tortured and executed horribly.

Elizabeth's cousin, Mary Queen of Scots, fled from Scotland when the Scots wanted rid of her. Elizabeth promised Mary a home in England. She first gave her a prison and then she had her beheaded … very messily.

Elizabeth was queen in an age when her sailors crossed the world to rob the Spanish of their gold. When the Spanish sent their huge fleet of ships, the 'Armada', for revenge it was Elizabeth's sailors who defended England.

Elizabeth had many 'favourites' but never married.

There were many plots to assassinate her but they were all discovered by Elizabeth's spies and the plotters usually died a slow and painful death.

She thought her enemies were out to kill her so she walked around the palace waving a rusty sword. When she fell ill she refused to let the doctors put her to bed because she thought she'd never get up alive. They propped her up on cushions. Her hands swelled up and her coronation ring had to be sawn off her finger before it cut into the flesh.

❋ Elizabeth's navy didn't defeat the Armada ships from Spain. Most of the Spanish ships were destroyed by fierce storms and she was never in any real danger. When the Armada was blown away and she felt safe, Elizabeth met her soldiers and sailors at the docks. She made a famous speech in which she said she was ready to die for them. She said she was as tough as any man ...

> 'I KNOW I HAVE THE BODY OF A WEAK, FEEBLE WOMAN – BUT I HAVE THE HEART AND STOMACH OF A KING.'

❋ But when the sailors suffered hunger and plague, Elizabeth left them to die in the streets.

If the diseases didn't get you then the captain might. Captains ruled their crews like cruel teachers:

❋ Swearing or cursing might earn you a one penny fine.
❋ Sleeping on duty or stealing could get you a ducking in the icy ocean.

❋ Disobey a captain's order? Then you might be tied to the mast and flogged.
❋ If you hit an officer, the hand that struck the blow might be sliced off ... if you were lucky. Some captains would simply hang you.

❋ Elizabeth had smallpox and the disease left her with a rough skin. She started to whiten her skin and hide her scars with a mixture of egg, powdered eggshells, poppy seeds and white lead. White lead is a poisonous powder. It ate into her skin, so she had to put on more and more layers. It seeped into her blood and her hair began to thin, which meant she had to wear a huge, spangled red wig. With her white face and curly red hair she looked more like a clown than a queen.

Potty poem

'I have the body of a feeble woman,' Queen Liz said (she wasn't too tall). 'I've the heart and stomach of any man.' (But the hair of a billiard ball.)

JAMES I

(1603–1625)

The crown went to James VI of Scotland, who became the first king to rule both England and Scotland. He was James I in England AND James VI in Scotland. But he never went back to Scotland so he never got mixed up ...

Famous for ...

... NOT being blown up by Guy Fawkes' gunpowder plot. He had promised he would be kinder to Catholics. He broke his promise so the Catholics set out to blow him and his lords to pieces.

FOUL FACTS

❀ James was afraid of witches. He watched some Scottish witches tortured with ...

Pilliwinks – screws on the thumbs
Cashielaws – a hot iron case around the leg
The Boot – an iron foot-crusher
Heid-rope – a tight knotted rope round the skull

❀ A visitor to England wrote about James ...

'HIS TONGUE WAS TOO LARGE FOR HIS MOUTH, WHICH MADE HIM DRINK VERY BADLY AS IF EATING HIS DRINK WHICH CAME OUT INTO THE CUP FROM EACH SIDE OF HIS MOUTH. HIS SKIN WAS SOFT BECAUSE HE NEVER WASHED HIS HANDS, ONLY RUBBED HIS FINGER ENDS SLIGHTLY WITH THE WET END OF A NAPKIN.'

Potty poem

Remember, remember, the fifth of November.
Gunpowder, treacherous games.
Now every November, Guy Fawkes is remembered,
But no one remembers old James.

TOP 10: SAVAGE SCOTTISH RULERS

Scotland had some leaders who were just as horrible as the English ones. Here's a top ten...

1. KENNETH II (971–995)

An old story says he killed the son of a witch called Finella. She invited Kenneth to take a gift: a statue that held a golden apple. When he grasped the apple it set off a machine that fired an arrow that killed him. Revenge.

2. MACBETH (1040–1057)

Macbeth is famous because William Shakespeare wrote a play about him 550 years later. Shakespeare said Macbeth invited King Duncan to his palace, waited till Duncan fell asleep, crept into Duncan's bedroom and stabbed the old man to death. Years later Macbeth's enemies, led by dead Duncan's son, attacked him at Dunsinane Castle and cut off his head. But the TRUTH is Shakespeare got it all wrong. Duncan wasn't an old man. He was 39 years old and younger than Macbeth. He didn't go to Macbeth's castle as a guest. They met in battle where Macbeth killed Duncan. And Macbeth didn't die at Dunsinane. He lost the Battle of Dunsinane but didn't die for another three years.

3. WILLIAM WALLACE (1297–1298)

WILLIAM WALLACE

MACBETH

William was a rebel leader who defeated Edward I's English invaders. Scotland had no king of its own. An English story said that Wallace killed Hugh Cressingham in the Battle of Stirling Bridge. The Scots leader stripped the skin off Cressingham and made it into a belt for his sword. Other bits of skin were turned into girths for the Scottish horses or sent around Scotland to boast of the victory. Of course the skinning of Cressingham could just be an English horror story. But it is true that the English Sheriff of Clydesdale torched Wallace's house and that Wallace's revenge was to murder him.

4. ROBERT BRUCE
(1306–1329)

Hunted by the English, Robert spent years battling to win his kingdom. There is the famous story about how Bruce spent one night, cold and tired, hiding in a cave in the Galloway hills. He had failed six times and was ready to give up. Then, by the light of his fire, he saw a spider swinging backwards and forwards from the ceiling, trying to reach the wall. It failed six times. At last it succeeded. 'If a

spider can try and try again, then so can I,' Bruce cried. He carried on and was greeted by the news that Edward, The Hammer of the Scots, had died. He won with his seventh try, just like the spider.

ROBERT BRUCE

Prince James was just 12 years old when he was captured by pirates in 1406. The pirates sold the prince to the enemy, Henry IV, who kept him prisoner in England. James's father died of a broken heart, and James became King of Scotland while still Henry's prisoner. Eventually, after 17 years in captivity, James was set free for money – a ransom. When James finally got back to Scotland he survived just 15 years before he was assassinated – by a Scot.

James II was in a battle, standing beside a cannon, when the cannon exploded, blew off his leg and killed him. He was a spoilsport king who banned football and golf in 1457. He said …

'IF THE MEN WANT TO PRACTISE A SPORT THEN THEY SHOULD TRY SOMETHING USEFUL, LIKE ARCHERY.'

7. JAMES III
(1460–1488)

King James III fought in the Battle of Sauchieburn and lost. In the battle he was wounded, but he'd probably have lived. Then a priest arrived to help the king. He 'helped' James into the afterlife by stabbing him to death. The priest turned out to be a soldier in disguise.

8. JAMES IV
(1488–1513)

Scotland's James IV was the last king in Britain to die in battle. Don't feel too sorry for him. It was James IV who had fought against James III at Sauchieburn, which led to the death of James III. And James III was his dad!

JAMES IV

106

10. JAMES VI
(1567–1625)

James VI of Scotland became James I of England. He wore a thickly padded jacket because he was scared of being stabbed. James VI wanted to marry Anne of Denmark. James sailed from Scotland for the wedding. He decided it would be wonderful wedding fun to have African dancers perform outdoors: he thought their dark skins would look awesome against the snow … but only if they wore very few clothes, of course. The dance was a great success – but not for the dancers. All four Africans caught pneumonia and died.

9. JAMES V
(1513–1542)

This James loved a sport called 'hurley hackett' or summer sledging. To play this, take a dead horse and boil its head till the flesh drops off. Take the clean skull to Heading Hill in Stirling. Use the skull as a sledge and race down the hill.

CHARLES I

(1625–1649)

James I's son took the throne, but it was a disaster for him and for England. There was a Civil War, with English killing English.

Famous for ...

... starting a war amongst his own people. Charles and his friends, the Cavaliers, went to war with the English Parliament, the Roundheads. When Charles was defeated, the Roundheads made him a 'no-head' when they gave him the chop.

FOUL FACTS

✿ Charles I didn't really expect to be king. His older brother, Henry, was the first in line to the throne. But Henry fell ill with typhus. Doctors suggested a cure of pigeons pecking at the bottom of his feet. Surprise, surprise, Henry died.

✿ After his execution, Charles's head was sewn back onto his body so his family could say goodbye to his corpse before it was buried.

✿ The neck bone of Charles I which suffered the chop was later taken from the tomb by Sir Henry Halford. He shocked friends at the dinner table by using it as a salt cellar.

Potty poem

'God saves this gracious king,'
That's what King Charles would sing,
'God saves this king.'
Roundheads said, 'With respect,
God is much more select.
He'll never, never save your neck.'
And they slayed the king.

CHARLES I

TOP 50

CHARLES II

(1660–1685)

Parliament ruled without a king for ten years. But the people decided they liked having a king so they invited chopped Charlie's son to take to the throne.

Famous for ...

... being jolly! Charles was called 'The Merry Monarch' because he enjoyed himself so much. It wasn't so much fun for the people who suffered from his cruelty. The English paid terrible taxes so Charles could have a great time.

Charles was king when London faced two disasters: the Great Plague in 1665 followed by the Great Fire of London the next year.

FOUL FACT

Charles II took his revenge on the men who had executed his father. They were hanged till they were half dead, had their guts pulled out and thrown onto a fire, then their bodies were cut into quarters. The leader of Charles I's enemies had been Oliver Cromwell. He was already dead and buried, so Charles II had his body dug up and his head cut off.

Potty poem

'It's being cheerful keeps me going,' Charles the Second said.
'Me dad was such a misery that they cut off his head.
Ha! You have to laugh.'
'And since I've been upon the throne we've had some fun!' he said.
'Except in 1665 ... the plague left thousands dead.
Ha! You have to laugh.
And then the countless thousands lost their homes in London's Fire;
Still, their merry monarch's here to raise their spirits higher.
Ha! They had some laughs.'

JAMES II
(1685–1688)

Charles II had no children so the throne went to his brother, James.

Famous for …

… running away to France. James was a Catholic and the English people were afraid of the Catholics ruling. The people rebelled and James was thrown out after three years. He fled to France. He sailed to Ireland and tried to start a war against England. He lost and ran back to France.

FOUL FACTS

✹ James II had the Duke of Monmouth's head chopped off for leading a rebellion. Monmouth gave the executioner six guineas so the man wouldn't make a mess of it.

✹ The executioner chopped – and missed. After a few goes he eventually got the head off. The executioner didn't give the duke his six guineas back.

✹ James started the war in Ireland and the Irish suffered horribly. He ran off and saved himself. The Irish were bitter and in their own language called him Séamus an Chaca or 'James the Poo'.

Potty poem

Dim Jim.
No one liked him
Chances very slim Jim,
So they threw him
Out. Jim
Never showed a glim-
-mer of any sense. Sim-
-ply had to go, Jim.

WILLIAM III

(1688–1702

& MARY II

The crown went to James's daughter, Mary. She shared it with William of Orange, her Dutch husband.

Famous for …

… the Glorious Revolution. In 1688 William landed with an army of 14,000 troops carried in 460 ships. The English navy and army didn't try to stop them. It is known as 'the Glorious Revolution' because James II ran away and no-one was hurt.

🌸 Mary II died of smallpox in 1694.

🌸 William was out riding one day in 1702 when his horse, Sorrel, stumbled on a molehill. The king fell off and broke his collarbone. The injury became infected and William died. The followers of his enemy, James, were thrilled. They thought the mole that dug the hole that killed the king was a wonderful creature. Ever since, the supporters of the Stuart family have drunk the health of 'the little gentleman in black velvet' – the mole.

🌸 William was small. Mary was large. She didn't take his arm when they walked together. Instead he took her arm. Someone said,

Potty poem

Lavender's blue, Orange Billy,
Lavender's green.
When you are king, Orange Billy,
Mary shall be queen.

'HE HUNG ON HER ARM LIKE A BRACELET.'

WILLIAM III & MARY II

TOP
50

ANNE

(1702–1714)

When William died, the throne passed to the last of the Stuarts – Mary II's sister, Anne.

Famous for …

… being the first monarch to see a single parliament for both England and Scotland. Her general, the Duke of Marlborough, won some glorious victories for her. She sacked him.

FOUL FACTS

🌸 Anne had 17 children. They all died as babies except one, William. When William reached the age of 11 he died too.

🌸 Anne was a large lady and suffered from gout – painful feet. She was the only monarch who had to be carried to her coronation.

🌸 She was known as Brandy Nan because she liked the drink, but it made her fat. When she died her body had swollen so large that she was buried in a coffin that was almost square.

I'M TOO FAT TO GO BACK IN THE BOTTLE

Potty poem

Anne was big, it has to be said.
Seventeen kids, all of them dead.
Miserable monarch up to the end.
Left without heirs, without husband or friends.

ANNE

CREAK

TOP 50

GEORGE I

(1714–1727)

As Anne had no children, the crown went to the great-grandson of James I. George was a German prince, the first of the Georgians.

Famous for …

… being King of England but never speaking the language. He had his wife, Sophia Dorothea, imprisoned in the palace of Ahlden Castle, Germany, and she was banned from seeing her children – George and Sophia Dorothea – ever again.

FOUL FACTS

✹ George I married Sophia Dorothea. He had lots of girlfriends and he thought that was alright. Then he heard that

Sophia Dorothea had a boyfriend. That was most definitely not alright. The man she had been flirting with was the handsome Count Konigsmark. Prince George ordered the count to leave the country the next day and never return. He was never seen again … alive.

✹ George had Sophia Dorothea kept a prisoner in the palace. Later, much later, after George and Sophia Dorothea died, the palace was rebuilt. Count Konigsmark was finally seen again after all those years. Where? His corpse was underneath the floorboards of Sophia Dorothea's dressing room.

Potty poem

We are the Germans and we're coming here to reign;
Never mind the language, never mind the pain.
Sophia Dorothea's keen … but you won't be seeing her.
Or would you like those Stuarts back? Which do you prefer?

GEORGE II

(1727–1760)

After George I came the second in a quaint quartet of German Georges.

Famous for …

… being the last British king to go to war himself. He led his troops into battle against the Prussians and the French. George hated his father because of the way he treated his mother, Sophia Dorothea. He is also famous for dying on the toilet.

FOUL FACTS

🌼 George II ordered the last ever beheading at the Tower of London. Lord Lovat was 80 years old and had supported a Stuart rebellion so he had to go. Lovat planned to enjoy his execution. He shouted insults to the crowd on his way to the scaffold. A stand was built for spectators. It collapsed under the weight of so many people. Twenty people were crushed to death in the collapse.

🌼 An English lady once visited George II in Germany. She found George's wife, Queen Caroline, whipping one of their children. 'Ah,' George said, 'you English have no good manners because you are not brought up properly.' The whipping was George's idea of bringing children up 'properly'.

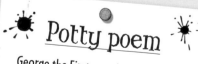

Potty poem

George the First was always reckoned
Bad, but worse was George the Second.
As for Caroline, his queen,
She's the worstest that there's been.

GEORGE III
(1760–1820)

George II's son, Frederick, died when he was hit by a cricket ball. The crown passed to George II's grandson, George III, who became the first king of Britain and Ireland.

Famous for …

… episodes of madness. During these times, his son took over as 'Prince Regent'. George III's Britain went to war with the United States of America after an argument about taxes. The Americans won and broke free of British rule.

FOUL FACTS

🟐 An assassin tried to shoot George III while he was at the theatre. The man fired two shots. Both missed by inches and the bullets ended in the wood panel behind the king. What did George do after this near miss? He stayed at the theatre and dropped off to sleep.

🟐 Stories went around about George's mental illness. There was one person who spread the worst lies and rumours about George III's madness – his own son, Prince George. The Prince would go around London clubs telling tales of his father's illness and even acting out the stories of his sick father.

Potty poem

People said that George the Third
Was not all there – in fact quite bonkers
Shook hands with a chestnut tree,
Got his head rained on by conkers.
But, if truth were told (that's best),
He was no worse than all the rest.

GEORGE IV

(1820–1830)

Prince George had waited a long time to get the crown, so he was going to enjoy himself now he finally had all that cash.

Famous for ...

... spending money. He rebuilt Buckingham Palace and Windsor Castle, which are still used by the royal family today. He grew so fat the rhyme 'Georgie Porgy pudding and pie' was written about him.

FOUL FACTS

🐾 George IV hated his wife, Caroline. He tried to divorce her, but wasn't allowed to. Caroline fell ill at the same time as the Emperor Napoleon became ill. The dramatic news was brought by a messenger:

> 'CONGRATULATIONS, SIRE, YOUR GREATEST ENEMY IS DEAD.'
> 'IS SHE REALLY?' GEORGE ASKED.

The messenger shook his puzzled head. It was Napoleon who had died. Caroline had another three months to go!

🐾 George IV once ate three pigeons and three beef steaks, washed down with a bottle of wine, a glass of champagne, two glasses of port and a glass of brandy ... and that was just his breakfast in bed. (It was his death-bed, as it happened.)

Potty poem

Georgie Porgy, pudding and pie
Kissed the girls and made them cry.
Kissing girls and drinking wine
Went on though he wed Caroline.

WILLIAM IV
(1830–1837)

George IV's daughter died, so the crown passed to his younger brother, William.

Famous for ...

... his time in the navy. William IV never expected to become king. When he was 13 he was sent off to join the navy and fought against the French and the Americans. His nickname was the 'Sailor King'.

FOUL FACTS

🍂 The British merchants were making a lot of money from the slave trade. William Wilberforce wanted to ban slavery. King William IV thought slavery was just fine and tried to stop Wilberforce.

🍂 William's wife was called Adelaide, and the Australian city was named after her. She had lived through the days of the French Revolution when the king, the queen and hundreds of nobles went to the chopping machine – the guillotine. Adelaide lived in fear that one day revolution would come to Britain and she would be beheaded.

Potty poem

What shall we do with a drunken sailor?
What shall we do with a drunken sailor?
What shall we do with a drunken sailor?
Crown him King William the Fourth as a matter of fact.

WILLIAM IV

TOP 50

VICTORIA

(1837–1901)

Victoria, William IV's, niece was just 18 when she became queen. She would reign on and on ...

What's her **story?**

Victoria ruled while the British Empire grew. She was made Empress of India and reigned over one quarter of all the people in the world. For all the riches this brought to Britain, many people in her home country lived terrible lives in slums.

And being Empress of India didn't make Queen Vic happy either. Her husband, Albert, died and she spent the rest of her life feeling sorry for herself. Albert was dead, but Victoria still made her servants lay out clean clothes for him every morning. It was as if he

were alive and going to wake up and get dressed. This went on for 40 years.

❧ While many poor British people starved, Victoria grew fatter and fatter. Her doctor said she looked like a barrel. A Victorian feast would have fed a poor family for weeks. Here are two real meals ...

Queen Victoria's feast (570 people):

220 serving bowls of soup
45 dishes of shellfish
2 sides of beef
10 sirloins, rumps and ribs of beef
50 boiled turkeys with oysters
80 pheasants
60 pigeon pies
45 decorated hams
140 jellies
200 ice creams
40 dishes of tarts
100 pineapples
Various other dishes
Champagnes and wines

Total: £8,172.25

Robert Crick's family (7 people):

Bread
Potatoes
Tea
Sugar
Salt
Butter
Cheese

Total: 55p

❧ People too poor to feed themselves were sent to the workhouses, where they were forced to slave for a little food.

🌸 The most famous writer in Victoria's reign was Charles Dickens. He told a tale of the workhouse in his book *Oliver Twist*.

> 'EACH BOY HAD ONE BOWL, AND NO MORE. THE BOWLS NEVER WANTED WASHING. THE BOYS POLISHED THEM WITH THEIR SPOONS TILL THEY SHONE AGAIN. AT LAST THEY BECAME SO HUNGRY THAT ONE BOY HINTED TO HIS FRIENDS THAT, IF HE DIDN'T GET ANOTHER BOWL OF GRUEL, HE WAS AFRAID HE MIGHT HAPPEN TO EAT THE BOY WHO SLEPT NEXT TO HIM. HE HAD A WILD, HUNGRY EYE, AND THEY BELIEVED HIM.'

🌸 One workhouse job was scraping rotten butcher's bones clean. A report described a true scene that was even worse than Dickens's tale ...

> 'THE BONE PICKERS ARE THE DIRTIEST OF ALL THE INMATES OF OUR WORKHOUSE – I HAVE SEEN THEM TAKE A BONE FROM THE DUNG HEAP AND CHEW IT WHILE REEKING HOT WITH DECAY. THESE CREATURES ARE OFTEN HARDLY HUMAN IN APPEARANCE,

> THEY HAVE NO HUMAN TASTES OR UNDERSTANDING, NOR EVEN HUMAN FEELINGS, FOR THEY ENJOYED THE FILTH WHICH WE EXPECT TO SEE IN DOGS AND OTHER LOWER ANIMALS BUT WHICH IS SICKENING TO US.'

🌸 The Irish suffered a terrible famine when their potato crops were ruined by a disease. Victoria visited the starving people but they didn't like seeing such a fat lady cheered by such skinny children. They called her the 'Famine Queen'.

🌸 Of course many poor people hated the Queen. There were SEVEN men who tried to assassinate her.

Potty poem

As a queen
Vic was mean.
Always fat, never lean.
Fell for Bert when nineteen,
When he died she weren't seen
For some years. She weren't keen.
Dreadful wars (like Crimean),
Awful slums (water green),
For the poor, not a bean.
That's the scene,
Victorean.

EDWARD VII

(1901–1910)

Victoria married Albert and the royal family name was Saxe-Coburg-Gotha. The only king to rule with that name was her son, Edward VII.

Famous for …

… waiting for the crown! Edward waited so long for his mother to die he thought he'd never become king. He spent his life as Prince of Wales chasing women, hunting, eating and gambling.

FOUL FACTS

🟥 Victoria and Albert decided their son, Edward, should not grow up spoiled. They told his teachers to be harsh with him and they showed him very little love themselves. They worried that he was a dimwit. The tough teaching didn't work. Edward grew up a greedy bully and never changed.

🟥 When he was 17 he tormented his man-servant by pouring hot wax over his new uniform, pouring water over his clean shirt and punching him on the nose.

🟥 When Edward VII came to the throne in 1901 he was the first monarch to have a beard since Charles I – the king who had his hair trimmed by the headsman's axe in 1649. No king had risked wearing a beard since. (And no queen either!)

Potty poem

Ed the Seven was fat, with a beard,
But not jolly as he had appeared.
Dad and Mum (Bert and Vic)
Thought their son was quite thick,
And they say that's what made him so weird.

GEORGE V

(1910–1936)

George, one of Queen Victoria's grandsons, took the British crown next. Other grandsons ruled Germany and Russia. One big family should have made for peace. It didn't.

Famous for …

… ruling the country during the First World War (1914–1918), which he fought against his cousin, Kaiser Wilhelm of Germany. George dropped the name Saxe-Coburg-Gotha because it sounded like the German enemy. The family took the name Windsor, which they still use today.

FOUL FACTS

✸ In 1917 the Russian people decided to get rid of Tsar Nicholas. Nicholas sent a message to George: 'Can my Russian royal family come to Britain for our safety, please?' If George had said 'Yes', then cousin Nicholas and his family could have been saved. But George refused. The Russian rebel army captured Nicholas and his family. They massacred them all, including the children.

Potty poem

'G is for German, Like Georgie our king!'
'A German! A German? I am no such thing.'
'Your Gran was Saxe-Coburg and you are the same.'
'Ja! Ja! … I mean, yes! yes! But what's in a name?'
'We can't have a German king. You'll have to go.'
'On nein! nein! my people … I mean, no, no, no!'
'The Kaiser's your cousin. To us that's a sin, sir.'
'Well, how would it be if we call ourselves …
Windsor?'

EDWARD VIII

(1936)

English kings and queens had died – some of them horribly – or been overthrown. But hardly any had simply given up. Edward VIII did.

Famous for …

… quitting his job as king. Edward fell in love with an American woman called Wallis Simpson. She had been married and divorced. She was still married to husband number two. In 1936 that was a shocking thing. The government told Edward he couldn't marry Wallis and stay on as king. He had to choose: Wallis or the crown. He chose Wallis.

FOUL FACTS

❀ An Irish fortune teller called Cheiro looked into the future, 11 years before Edward became king. He said …

> 'EDWARD WILL FALL VICTIM OF A SHOCKING LOVE AFFAIR. IF HE DOES THEN I SEE THAT THE PRINCE WILL GIVE UP EVERYTHING – EVEN THE CHANCE OF BEING CROWNED – RATHER THAN LOSE HIS LOVE.'

❀ He was right. On 11 December 1936 Edward gave up the crown. But Cheiro didn't cheer … he had died eight weeks before. Bet he didn't see that coming!

Potty poem

'I'm proud to be your king and I
Will serve you till the day I die …
But hang on chaps! Just tell me why
I can't have Wallis? Think I'll cry
Boo! Hoo! And stuff your throne. Goodbye.'

GEORGE VI

(1936–1952)

George VI was one of those princes who didn't expect to become king.

Famous for …

… being king when Britain fought the Second World War (1939–1945). He had been in the navy and fought at the Battle of Jutland in the First World War. Once he became king he was not allowed to fight again. George VI was having tea in Buckingham Palace when it was bombed in 1940.

FOUL FACTS

✺ George VI enjoyed hunting and was so keen he kept a detailed diary of all of his kills. His last diary entry said he'd killed a hare running at full speed. That pleased him. Just as well, because it was his last shot. A few hours later he was dead himself.

✺ George VI stammered. His daughter, Elizabeth II, believes that it was because he was treated too strictly by his teachers. George VI also suffered bullying as a naval cadet. It's said that royal people have 'blue blood'. George's fellow cadets used to prick him with pins to see if his blood did run blue. (It never did.)

Potty poem

You're king!
I'm what?
You're king!
I'm not!
King Ed …
Not dead?
He's gone.
Get that crown on.
Take off that hat.
I'm really king? Well, fancy that!

ELIZABETH II

(1952–?)

Elizabeth was young when she took the throne and she has ruled for over 60 years. It looks as if she will overtake Victoria to reign longer than any other monarch in the history of Britain.

Famous for …

… Victoria built up the huge British Empire. Elizabeth watched many of the nations leave the Empire.

FOUL FACTS

Of all the monarchs in all the palaces in all of Britain, Elizabeth was the one who said:

> 'THERE'S TOO MUCH, YOU KNOW, HISTORY!'

Elizabeth II married Prince Philip of Greece and Denmark. She kept the family name 'Windsor'. Prince Philip grumbled …

> 'I AM THE ONLY MAN IN THE COUNTRY NOT ALLOWED TO GIVE HIS NAME TO HIS OWN CHILDREN.'

Potty poem

Remember the curse on the number two?
How Georgie the Second died on the loo,
How Richard the Second met his sorry death;
How someone stopped Edward the Two's little breath,
While Charlie the Second faced fires and plague,
And William the Second didn't die of old age.
Now Lizzie the Second could beat twos of the past
If of all the Brit Monarchs she is simply … the last.

INDEX